FAVORITE RECIPES

W9-AJT-908

COOKING WITH
Refrigerated Dough

CONTENTS

QUICK CHOCOLATE CHIP STICKY BUNS

MAKES 8 STICKY BUNS

2 tablespoons butter

1 package (11 ounces) refrigerated French bread dough

¼ cup sugar

1 teaspoon ground cinnamon

½ cup mini semisweet chocolate chips

⅓ cup pecan pieces, toasted*

1 tablespoon maple syrup

To toast pecans, spread on ungreased baking sheet. Bake in preheated 350°F oven 6 to 8 minutes or until golden brown, stirring frequently.

1. Preheat oven to 350°F. Place butter in 9-inch round cake pan; place pan in oven while preheating to melt butter.

2. Meanwhile, unroll dough on cutting board. Combine sugar and cinnamon in small bowl; sprinkle evenly over dough. Top with chocolate chips. Starting with short side, roll up dough jelly-roll style. Cut crosswise into eight slices with serrated knife.

3. Remove pan from oven. Stir pecans and maple syrup into melted butter; mix well. Arrange dough slices cut sides up in pan, pressing gently into pecan mixture.

4. Bake 20 to 22 minutes or until golden brown. Immediately invert pan onto serving plate; scrape any pecans or butter mixture remaining in pan onto buns. Serve warm.

PEPPERONI BREAD

MAKES ABOUT 6 SERVINGS

1 package
(about 14 ounces)
refrigerated
pizza dough

8 slices provolone
cheese

20 to 30 slices
pepperoni (about
half of 6-ounce
package)

½ teaspoon Italian
seasoning

¾ cup (3 ounces)
shredded
mozzarella
cheese

½ cup grated
Parmesan cheese

1 egg, beaten

Marinara sauce,
heated

1. Preheat oven to 400°F. Unroll dough on sheet of parchment paper with long side facing you. Cut off corners of dough to create large oval shape.

2. Arrange half of provolone slices over bottom half of oval, cutting to fit as necessary. Top with pepperoni; sprinkle with ¼ teaspoon Italian seasoning. Top with mozzarella, Parmesan and remaining provolone slices; sprinkle with remaining Italian seasoning.

3. Fold top half of dough over filling to create half moon (calzone) shape; press edges with fork or pinch edges to seal. Transfer calzone with parchment paper to large baking sheet; curve slightly into crescent shape. Brush with beaten egg.

4. Bake about 16 minutes or until crust is golden brown. Remove to wire rack to cool slightly. Cut crosswise into slices; serve warm with marinara sauce for dipping.

COOKIE DOUGH MONKEY BREAD

MAKES ABOUT 16 SERVINGS

1 package (about 16 ounces) break-apart refrigerated chocolate chip cookie dough (24 cookies)

2 packages (7½ ounces each) refrigerated buttermilk biscuits (10 biscuits per package)

1 cup semisweet chocolate chips, divided

¼ cup whipping cream

1. Preheat oven to 350°F. Generously spray 12-cup (10-inch) bundt pan with nonstick cooking spray.

2. Break cookie dough into 24 pieces; split each piece in half to create total of 48 pieces. Separate biscuits; cut each biscuit into four pieces with scissors. Layer half of cookie dough and half of biscuit pieces in prepared pan, alternating doughs. Sprinkle with ¼ cup chocolate chips. Repeat layers with remaining cookie dough and biscuit pieces; sprinkle with ¼ cup chocolate chips.

3. Bake 27 to 30 minutes or until biscuits are golden brown, covering loosely with foil during last 10 minutes of baking. Remove pan to wire rack; let stand, covered, 5 minutes. Loosen edges of bread with knife; invert onto serving plate.

4. Pour cream into medium microwavable bowl; microwave on HIGH 1 minute or until simmering. Add remaining ½ cup chocolate chips; stir until chocolate is melted. Let stand 5 minutes to thicken slightly. Drizzle glaze over bread.

8

BBQ CHICKEN STROMBOLI

MAKES 6 SERVINGS

1 rotisserie-roasted chicken* (2 to 2¼ pounds)

⅓ cup barbecue sauce

1 package (about 14 ounces) refrigerated pizza dough

1 cup (4 ounces) shredded Cheddar cheese

⅓ cup sliced green onions, divided

Or substitute 8 ounces deli roast chicken breast, chopped.

1. Remove and discard chicken skin and bones. Shred meat into bite-size pieces. (You should have about 4 cups shredded chicken.) Combine 2 cups chicken and barbecue sauce in medium bowl; stir to coat. Wrap and refrigerate or freeze remaining chicken for another use.

2. Preheat oven to 400°F. Spray baking sheet with nonstick cooking spray. Unroll dough on baking sheet; pat into 12×9-inch rectangle.

3. Spread chicken mixture lengthwise down center of dough, leaving 2½ inches on each side. Sprinkle with cheese and ¼ cup green onions. Fold long sides of dough over filling; press edges to seal. Sprinkle with remaining green onions.

4. Bake 19 to 22 minutes or until golden brown. Let stand 10 minutes before slicing.

APPLE BERRY CINNAMON ROLL SKILLET COBBLER

MAKES 8 SERVINGS

1 tablespoon cornstarch

2 tablespoons lemon juice

5 apples (about 2 pounds), peeled and cut into ½-inch pieces

½ cup packed brown sugar

¾ teaspoon ground cinnamon

⅛ teaspoon ground ginger

3 tablespoons butter

½ cup coarsely chopped pecans

1 cup fresh blueberries

1 package (13 ounces) refrigerated flaky cinnamon rolls with icing

1. Preheat oven to 350°F.

2. Stir cornstarch into lemon juice in small bowl until smooth. Combine apples, brown sugar, cinnamon and ginger in large bowl; mix well. Add cornstarch mixture; toss to coat.

3. Melt butter in large ovenproof skillet over medium heat. Add apple mixture and pecans; press into single layer to cover bottom of skillet. Sprinkle with blueberries.

4. Bake 20 minutes. Separate cinnamon rolls; reserve icing. Arrange cinnamon rolls over warm fruit mixture.

5. Bake 20 to 25 minutes or until filling is bubbly and cinnamon rolls are deep golden brown. Drizzle with icing. Let stand 5 minutes before serving.

SPICY BEEF TURNOVERS

MAKES 10 APPETIZERS

½ **pound ground beef or turkey**

2 **cloves garlic, minced**

2 **tablespoons soy sauce**

1 **tablespoon water**

½ **teaspoon cornstarch**

1 **teaspoon curry powder**

¼ **teaspoon Chinese five-spice powder**

¼ **teaspoon red pepper flakes**

2 **tablespoons minced green onion**

1 **package (7½ ounces) refrigerated buttermilk biscuits (10 biscuits)**

1 **egg**

1 **tablespoon water**

1. Preheat oven to 400°F. Line baking sheet with parchment paper or spray with nonstick cooking spray.

2. Cook beef and garlic in medium skillet over medium-high heat until beef is no longer pink, stirring to break up meat. Drain fat.

3. Whisk soy sauce and water into cornstarch in small bowl until smooth. Add soy sauce mixture, curry powder, five-spice powder and red pepper flakes to skillet; cook and stir 30 seconds or until liquid is absorbed. Remove from heat; stir in green onion.

4. Separate biscuits; roll each biscuit into 4-inch round between two sheets of waxed paper. Spoon heaping tablespoon beef mixture onto one side of each biscuit; fold dough over filling to form semicircle. Pinch edges together to seal. Place turnovers on prepared baking sheet. Beat egg and water in small bowl; brush lightly over turnovers.

5. Bake 9 to 10 minutes or until golden brown. Serve warm or at room temperature.

TIP: The turnovers may be wrapped before baking and frozen up to 3 months. Thaw completely before proceeding with baking as directed in step 5.

PUNCHED PIZZA ROUNDS

MAKES 20 APPETIZERS

1 package
(12 ounces)
refrigerated
flaky buttermilk
biscuits
(10 biscuits)

80 mini pepperoni
slices *or* 20 small
pepperoni slices

8 to 10 pickled
jalapeño pepper
slices, chopped
(optional)

1 tablespoon dried
basil

½ cup pizza sauce

1½ cups (6 ounces)
shredded
mozzarella
cheese

Shredded
Parmesan cheese
(optional)

1. Preheat oven to 400°F. Spray 20 standard (2½-inch) nonstick muffin cups with nonstick cooking spray.

2. Separate biscuits; split each biscuit in half horizontally to create 20 rounds. Place in prepared muffin cups. Press 4 mini pepperoni slices into center of each round. Sprinkle with jalapeños, if desired, and basil. Spread pizza sauce over pepperoni; sprinkle with mozzarella.

3. Bake 8 to 9 minutes or until bottoms of pizzas are golden brown. Sprinkle with Parmesan, if desired. Cool in pans 2 minutes; remove to wire racks. Serve warm.

APPLE PIE MONKEY BREAD

MAKES ABOUT 12 SERVINGS

½ cup (1 stick) butter, divided

2 large apples (about 1 pound), peeled and cut into ½-inch pieces (Fuji, Granny Smith or Braeburn)

½ cup plus 1 tablespoon sugar, divided

2½ teaspoons ground cinnamon, divided

½ cup finely chopped pecans

2 packages (7½ ounces each) refrigerated buttermilk biscuits (10 biscuits per package)

1. Preheat oven to 350°F. Spray 9-inch deep-dish pie plate with nonstick cooking spray.

2. Melt ¼ cup butter in large skillet or saucepan over medium heat. Add apples, 1 tablespoon sugar and ½ teaspoon cinnamon; cook and stir 5 minutes or until apples are tender and glazed. Transfer to large bowl. Melt remaining ¼ cup butter in same skillet, stirring to scrape up any glaze. Cool slightly.

3. Combine pecans, remaining ½ cup sugar and 2 teaspoons cinnamon in medium bowl. Separate biscuits; cut each biscuit into four pieces with scissors. Dip biscuit pieces in melted butter; roll in pecan mixture to coat. Place one quarter of biscuit pieces in prepared pie plate; top with one quarter of apples. Repeat layers three times. Sprinkle with remaining pecan mixture and drizzle with remaining butter.

4. Bake 30 minutes or until biscuits are firm and topping is golden brown. Serve warm.

SUPER SIMPLE CHEESY BUBBLE LOAF

MAKES 12 SERVINGS

2 packages (7½ ounces each) refrigerated buttermilk biscuits (10 biscuits per package)

2 tablespoons butter, melted

1½ cups (6 ounces) shredded Italian cheese blend

1. Preheat oven to 350°F. Spray 9×5-inch loaf pan with nonstick cooking spray.

2. Separate biscuits; cut each biscuit into four pieces with scissors. Layer half of biscuit pieces in prepared pan. Drizzle with 1 tablespoon butter; sprinkle with 1 cup cheese. Top with remaining biscuit pieces, 1 tablespoon butter and ½ cup cheese.

3. Bake about 25 minutes or until golden brown. Serve warm.

TIP: It's easy to change up the flavors in this simple bread. Try Mexican cheese blend instead of Italian, and add taco seasoning and/or hot pepper sauce to the melted butter before drizzling it over the dough. Or, sprinkle ¼ cup chopped ham, salami or crumbled crisp-cooked bacon between the layers of dough.

HAM AND SWISS TWISTS

MAKES ABOUT 22 TWISTS

1 package (about 14 ounces) refrigerated pizza dough

6 very thin slices Swiss cheese

6 very thin slices smoked ham

Black pepper

1. Preheat oven to 400°F. Line baking sheets with parchment paper.

2. Unroll dough on cutting board; press into 16×12-inch rectangle. Arrange single layer of cheese slices over half of dough, cutting slices to fit as necessary. Top with ham slices; sprinkle with pepper. Fold other half of dough over ham and cheese layers, creating 12×8-inch rectangle.

3. Cut dough into ½-inch strips (8 inches long). Twist strips several times; place on prepared baking sheets.

4. Bake about 14 minutes or until golden brown. Serve warm.

VARIATION: For added flavor, spread honey or Dijon mustard over dough before layering with cheese and ham. Serve with additional mustard for dipping.

NOTE: Ham and Swiss Twists are about 12 inches long. For smaller twists, cut in half after baking.

BARBECUE CHICKEN FLATBREAD

MAKES 4 SERVINGS

3 tablespoons red wine vinegar

2 teaspoons sugar

¼ red onion, thinly sliced (about ⅓ cup)

3 cups shredded rotisserie chicken

½ cup barbecue sauce

1 package (about 14 ounces) refrigerated pizza dough

All-purpose flour, for dusting

1½ cups (6 ounces) shredded mozzarella cheese

1 green onion, thinly sliced on bias

2 tablespoons chopped fresh cilantro

1. Place oven rack in lower third of oven. Preheat oven to 400°F. Line baking sheet with parchment paper.

2. Combine vinegar and sugar in small bowl; stir until sugar is dissolved. Add red onion; cover and let stand at room temperature while preparing flatbread.

3. Combine chicken and barbecue sauce in medium bowl; toss to coat.

4. Roll out dough into 11×9-inch rectangle on lightly floured surface. Transfer dough to prepared baking sheet; top with cheese and barbecue chicken mixture.

5. Bake about 12 minutes or until crust is golden brown and crisp and cheese is melted. Drain liquid from red onion; sprinkle over flatbread. Garnish with green onion and cilantro. Serve immediately.

BREAKFAST BISCUIT BAKE

MAKES 8 SERVINGS

8 ounces bacon, chopped

1 small onion, finely chopped

1 clove garlic, minced

¼ teaspoon red pepper flakes

5 eggs

¼ cup milk

½ cup (2 ounces) shredded white Cheddar cheese, divided

¼ teaspoon salt

⅛ teaspoon black pepper

1 package (16 ounces) refrigerated jumbo buttermilk biscuits (8 biscuits)

1. Preheat oven to 425°F. Cook bacon in large ovenproof skillet until crisp. Remove to paper towel-lined plate. Drain off and reserve drippings, leaving 1 tablespoon in skillet.

2. Add onion, garlic and red pepper flakes to skillet; cook and stir over medium heat 8 minutes or until onion is softened. Set aside to cool slightly.

3. Whisk eggs, milk, ¼ cup cheese, salt and black pepper in medium bowl until well blended. Stir in onion mixture.

4. Wipe out any onion mixture remaining in skillet; grease with additional bacon drippings, if necessary. Separate biscuits and arrange in single layer in bottom of skillet. (Bottom of skillet should be completely covered.) Pour egg mixture over biscuits; sprinkle with remaining ¼ cup cheese and cooked bacon.

5. Bake about 25 minutes or until puffed and golden brown. Serve warm.

MAPLE WALNUT APPLE CRESCENT COBBLER

MAKES 8 SERVINGS

Filling

6 Golden Delicious apples (2½ pounds), peeled and thinly sliced

⅓ cup maple syrup

2 tablespoons all-purpose flour

2 teaspoons vanilla

⅛ teaspoon ground nutmeg

Topping

1 package (8 ounces) refrigerated crescent roll dough

4 teaspoons butter, melted

¼ cup chopped walnuts

2 tablespoons packed brown sugar

1. Place oven rack in center of oven. Preheat oven to 375°F. Spray 8-inch square baking dish with nonstick cooking spray.

2. Combine apples, maple syrup, flour, vanilla and nutmeg in medium bowl; toss to coat. Spoon into prepared baking dish.

3. Bake 30 minutes or until apples are tender but still firm.

4. Meanwhile, divide dough into eight triangles; place on work surface. Brush top of each triangle with melted butter. Combine walnuts and brown sugar in small bowl; sprinkle over dough. Starting with wide end, roll up each dough triangle to form crescent. Arrange crescents in two rows over warm apple mixture.

5. Bake 15 minutes. Cover loosely with foil; bake 30 minutes. Uncover; bake 3 minutes or until filling is thick and bubbly and crescent rolls are golden brown.

PEPPERONI PIZZA DIPPERS

MAKES 4 SERVINGS

1 package (8 ounces) refrigerated crescent roll dough, preferably without seams

2 tablespoons marinara sauce, plus additional for dipping

4 tablespoons shredded mozzarella cheese

8 slices pepperoni

1. Preheat waffle maker to medium. Unroll dough on cutting board; cut into four rectangles.

2. Place one rectangle of dough on waffle maker; spread with 1 tablespoon sauce, leaving ½-inch border around edges. Top with 1 tablespoon cheese, 4 slices pepperoni, additional 1 tablespoon cheese and second rectangle of dough. Close waffle maker.

3. Cook about 8 minutes or until dough is cooked through and golden brown. Repeat with remaining dough, sauce, cheese and pepperoni. Serve warm with additional sauce for dipping.